Caps!

Written by Phoebe Wells

Here is a red cap.

Here is a blue cap.

Here is a fun cap.

4

Here is a little cap.

5

Here is a flap cap.

Here is a nap cap.

Caps! Caps! Caps!

Word Study

 cap

 flap

Can you read these words?

a   here   is   little

Stage 0/1
Book 8

DRA	3
Guided Reading	B
Intervention	3
Lexile Level	BR
Word Count	33

Modern
Curriculum
Press

Pearson Learning Group

ISBN 0-7652-1472-5

90000>

9 780765 214720